Enigma

Enigma

Poems

Anita Endrezze

Press 53
Winston-Salem

Press 53, LLC
PO Box 30314
Winston-Salem, NC 27130

First Edition

Silver Concho Poetry Series
edited by Pamela Uschuk and William Pitt Root

Copyright © 2019 by Anita Endrezze

All rights reserved, including the right of reproduction in whole or in part in any form except in the case of brief quotations embodied in critical articles or reviews. For permission, contact publisher at editor@Press53.com, or at the address above.

Cover design by Kevin Morgan Watson

Cover art, "The space of me is beyond me," Copyright © 2019 by Anita Endrezze, used by permission of the artist.

Library of Congress Control Number
2019935258

Printed on acid-free paper
ISBN 978-1-950413-04-1

to my family. . . and the crows

The author wishes to thank the publications where the following poems first appeared.

About Place: Dignity as an Endangered Species in the 21st Century, "Crows in color," "November," "Short of life"

Book View Café, Feb. 3, 2017 (via Ursula K. Le Guin), "The Wall"

Cutthroat: A Journal of the Arts, Issue 24, "How to Taste Chocolate," "Night Psalm," "Small Space," and "The Train Wreck of Love"

Gulf Coast, Issue 3.1, "The Immigrant Called Moon"

North American Review, Fall 2011, "Thirteen Ways of Looking at an Indian"

Truth To Power: Writers Respond to the Rhetoric of Hate and Fear (online version): "The Molotov Cocktail of Love and Fear," "Presidential Interview: The Donald of All Bombs" and "Enigmas"

Contents

The Wall	3
The Exile	5
The Immigrant Called Moon	6
Man Sets Underwear on Fire in Walmart	7
Enigmas	8
Presidential Interview: The Donald of All Bombs	9
Variation on the Word Falling	10
The Cocktail of Love and Fear	12
K.I.A.	14
Thirteen Ways of Looking at an Indian	16
Witchery	19
Earth Day	20
Twenty and One	22
From *Seattle Zine*	23
A Poem Not about the Bear	24
Black Crows on Green Cedar	26
Herons, Flying	27
Crows in Color	28
Twilight of the Dreams	29
April	31
rain the rain	32
13 Ways to Not Write a Poem	34
Dear poem,	36
Poem in a Pocket	38
My Own Oneness	39
Why I Don't Have Tattoos	40
A Teaspoon of Life	41
Relativity	42
No One Wants to Talk about This	43
Short of Life	44
Lessons My Mom Taught Me	45
The Train Wreck of Love	46

November	47
Somewhere It's Night	48
Small Space	49
A Symmetry of Eyebrows	51
How to Taste Chocolate	53
The Lost Umbrellas	54
The Sacred Dissolving	56
The Secret of Black	57
The Secret of Balloons	58
Collections	59
Noon	61
Cup	61
Roof	62
Passing	63
Circle	64
The Tunnel's Secret	65
A Circle Can't Have Corners	66
A Poem Found in a Dream	67
Night Psalm	68
The Secrets of Time	69
Author Biography	71

Enigma

The Wall

Build a wall of saguaros,
butterflies, and bones
of those who perished
in the desert. A wall of worn shoes,
dry water bottles, poinsettias.
Construct it of gilded or crazy house
mirrors so some can see their true faces.
Build a wall of revolving doors
or revolutionary *abuelas*.
Make it as high as the sun, strong as tequila.
Boulders of sugar skulls. Adobe or ghosts.
A Lego wall or bubble wrap. A wall of hands
holding hands, hair braided from one woman
to another, one country to another.
A wall made of Berlin. A wall made for tunneling.
A beautiful wall of taco trucks.
A wall of silent stars and migratory songs.
This wall of solar panels and holy light,
panels of compressed Cheetos,
topped not by barbed wire but sprouting
avocado seeds, those Aztec testicles.
A wall to keep Us in and Them out.
It will have faces and heartbeats.
Dreams will be terrorists. The Wall will divide
towns, homes, mountains,
the sky that airplanes fly through
with their potential illegals.
Our wallets will be on life support
to pay for it. Let it be built
of guacamole so we can have a bigly block party.
Mortar it with *xocoatl*, chocolate. Build it from coyote howls
and wild horses drumming across the plains of Texas,
from the memories
of hummingbird warriors and healers.
Stack it thick as blood, which has mingled
for centuries, *la vida*. Dig the foundation deep.
Create a 2,000-mile altar, lit with votive candles

for those who have crossed over
defending freedom under spangled stars
and drape it with rebozos,
and sweet grass.
Make it from two-way windows:
the wind will interrogate us,
the rivers will judge us, for they know how to separate
and divide to become whole.
Pink Floyd will inaugurate it.
Ex-Presidente Fox will give it the middle finger salute.
Wiley Coyote will run headlong into it,
and survive long after history forgets us.
Bees will find sand-scoured holes and fill them
with honey. Heroin will cover it in blood.
But it will be a beautiful wall. A huge wall.
Remember to put a rose-strewn doorway in Nogales
where my grandmother crossed over,
pistols on her hips. Make it a gallery of graffiti art,
a refuge for tumbleweeds,
a border of stories we already know by heart.

The Exile

She is from somewhere and lives everywhere.
She is misplaced,
remembering her old life
when everything made sense.
The flowers had familiar faces.
The butcher knew her name.
The cobble streets led her home
whichever door she opened.
Yes, there was hunger.
The old days were bones and bread.
And there was fear.
The boots in her dreams still crush her.
But it was a hunger she knew
and a fear she understood.
Now she's an undecipherable state
without words for the future
and the lines on her palm
are faint, without definition.
When she looks in a mirror,
her eyes shift to the strange light.
And her mouth opens O.
Her face is a map of a lost country.

The Immigrant Called Moon

Moon crosses the river
without any papers.
Moon dies of thirst in the desert.
Moon scrubs your toilets,
plucks oranges from trees.
Moon hides her Otherness under a bright scarf.
Moon eats food you can't pronounce
but you decide you like it anyway.
Moon is a doctor who saves you.
Moon is a singer who desires you.
Moon is a stranger in your own house.
Moon walks your uneasy streets.
Moon is murdered under the stars
and lies there, dimly glowing 'til dawn.
Moon is frightened by the knock at the door.
Moon marries your son and lives in bicultural compromise forever.
Moon becomes part of your family and you kiss her cheek at bedtime.
Moon dies one day, and suddenly, everyone realizes how life is darker
without Moon's fluid syllables and strange ways.
The light that was her eye
is the light that shines from each of us:
little orbs, little souls, crossing over, without boundaries.

Man Sets Underwear on Fire in Walmart

I have only gone to Walmart twice
because I'm a department store snob.
But wait I used to shop at Kmart.
Okay but I don't like Walmart
because their employees
don't get paid enough
which means they have to get charity turkeys
for Thanksgiving, or so I heard.
But I would go to Walmart
on the day a man falls asleep
on the can, smoking
a cigarette which sets his underwear on fire.
Not because I'm a mean person
(I don't want him to be hurt)
but it was an historic occasion.
Among all the Nation of the People of Walmart
he's the only one who got a headline.
You see pics of men in wife beaters
and tutus. You see a woman with a pink tail
peeking out from under her skirt.
She has a mohawk. A man in tie-dye
capris and tee, with yellow suspenders.
A man in high heels with a panda backpack.
A man with a cloth hot dog hat.
Butt cracks and big bellies.
But he's the only People of Walmart worthy
of a headline, a unique feat
in the bizarre world we all live in,
where children are bombed
and our president lives in a golden tower,
tweeting that his microwave could be a camera
and everyone lies   sad
and cake is beautiful but a child is an enemy,
and Mexicans are bad but tacos are good.
We see him with orange skin,
hair upswept in a platinum pompadour
like his mommy
and his baggy golf shorts
and we know the whole country
is now a Walmart,
a headline we all live in.

Enigmas

There are contradictions
in sunlight, the way it touches
a gassed child
as well as a yellow rose.

Everything is a riddle,
like turning your favorite shirt
inside out and finding
dark feathers.

This is my heart, a secret moon.
Distant blue mountains
float above the Salish Sea.
My shadow is growing old.

There is a paradox
in the water washing
the dead child
for the afterlife.

We are on our knees.
A puzzle with no solution.
We raise guns and aim.
We lift palms and pray.

A weary poem made of flesh
and bone.
Look into my eyes, beloved.
When does it end?

Presidential Interview: The Donald of All Bombs

1
The world is a beautiful chocolate cake.
Brilliant missiles light up the cake.

Fifty-nine missiles. Make a wish and blow
it all up. Grin and eat cake.

We need more bombs!
My factory makes 'em! Smash the cake!

Big bombs. Beautiful death. Hugely sums
of profit, icing on my cake.

NATO is not obsolete. China doesn't manipulate
currency but they make terrible terrible! rice cake.

Cut the arts! Cut the food programs!
It's not good for children and old people to eat cake.

2
After a weekend of golf and small balls,
let's send a 21,000 lb. non-nuclear bomb to cake

the whole area in blasted dust. My ratings
will go up bigly. I'll take ALL of the cake.

I don't have small hands. My bombs are huge.
Syria or Iraq or Afghanistan. Those people don't eat cake.

I won the election. The media is a stink bomb.
Obama hid "wiretaps" in my chocolate cake.

I'm President.
You're not. Don't eat my cake.

Variation on the Word Falling

Sometimes you fight the darkness.
His name is God or
a beautiful bomb.
He's muscular with teeth in his heart.
You fight. There's no vanity in fear.
Your mouth twists, drooling, stuttering
against the chemical warfare
in your brain. You fall
like lightning to the root.

Soldiers took away the horses
and slaughtered them.
You collapse, hearing hooves clacking
against stone. Bullets and sabers.
You raised that one since she wobbled
on spindly legs.
You fall to your knees,
weeping, holding the light
in the mare's eyes to the end.

You free-fall in love.
You walk unharmed from life's gallows.
You feel light-hearted even as love
wraps you in its straight jacket.
Then you fall out of love,
a butterfly with its wings
torn off one by one
by The One.

The child falls, the soldier falls, calling
for his mother. The knife falls from the fist;
the list of condemned
is the many names of god.
They are our names.
The variations of dark falling
is not the same as light rising.

We march against the armies
who follow the bullet-headed generals.
They about-face, aim and fire.
We fall and in falling, fall.
Our leaders own
the crows, the trees, the fiery air.
They own the fist and the darkness.
They own the fight, the black boots
that grind the bones.

We believed in the open window,
the goodness of birds singing
and life going on. We thought
we were stronger but
the leaders have grenades for hearts
and send the uniforms
to punch our guts with gusto.
Crows plummet from the trees
to feast on the light failing
in our eyes. Riderless horses gallop
in the war zone. That lover
was a lion I kissed. Now he's forgotten
his name, his mask. He's a nesting doll
of bones. Everything falls, every day withers.
A leaf without a tree.

The Cocktail of Love and Fear

Look, the stars are boxed up.
Even snow is in a glass globe.
You don't know the world.

Here, the seacalm is an iris blue field.
On the other side there was napalm
but I wasn't invited
to that party when everyone marched
over the water with their salt boots.

When I was young
I had a lover afraid of horses
and doors, so I made my moony body into a key
and lather-rode into his nightmares,
hoping he'd wake up love-brave.
But he left, fear spurring him.

If you open the box
and stars swarm out like bullets
I'll drink all your darkness deep.
I'll drink to forget how we lost the light.
I'll swallow ecstasy
until the world is turned twirly updown
and outside in.
How else to make sense
of this life when babies
are boiled by gas.

We hand wring our finger bones,
worrying about dictators with ego bombs.
The party is over. Or it's just begun.
The generals put on their party clothes.
Ships are at sea,
with penile missiles and stars that will explode
inside skin boxes
with foreign names.

Dictators are afraid of projectile dysfunction
and small small hands.
They know the world is up for grabs
yet fear fear they can't hold on.
They chew beautiful slices
of death.

The innocents scream prayers
but generals put the godspirit
in grenades. We're all in a dark place.
Boxes or coffins. See the ashes
swirling in this globe. Sand glowing
in the dark. Shit falling from the sky.

Everything has eyes. The heavens
with the stars of the dead,
the trees in roseate bomb light,
the grasses that grow from lost bones.
We thought love was stronger.
We see that life is a dirty bomb.

Damn the blind gods.

K.I.A.

> *We are all the children of one God. The sun, the darkness,*
> *the winds are all listening to what we have to say.*
> —Geronimo (Goyathlay)

The sun
is a prairie of light.

The darkness
listens to us
as we wonder
if it is separate
from ourselves.

The prairie moon
is yellow grass
and river stones.

The People sing
their voices
lost in the vastness.

Then comes the soldiers,
with orders to march on
boots heavy as centuries.

The silence of light.
Clouds of blasted flame.
The earth turns red.
Time passes from enemy
to enemy. Whose hands
are clean from the ashes
of the dead?

Tail winds of bombs,
bullets cracking
the sky
into our bones, your bones,
all the bones of the sky
breaking dawn
into splinters
of death.

*This poem was written in response to our government's code name for capturing Osama Bin Laden. The operation was called "Geronimo." It dishonored a Native American leader and shows that the government was comparing two enemies with little understanding of Native culture and history. After the Bin Laden raid was completed, they transmitted this message: "Geronimo EKIA," which means "Geronimo Enemy Killed In Action."

Thirteen Ways of Looking at an Indian

1
Among twenty Indians only one
has skin coppery as a penny
and she sprayed it on.

2
If you're a half-breed,
you're always of two minds
but your heart is Red.

3
Coyote whirls in dust devils,
grinning in the heart
of our stories.

4
A man and a woman
(or a man and a man
or a woman and a woman)
are one. A human and Coyote
are trouble.

5
I don't know which I prefer:
Native American, ndn, Indian.
Skins or sly innuendos from Coyote
as he saunters down the street,
whistling, "Yo, *mamacita*, you bad honey!"

6
I grew up half white, but
Coyote's shadow is moody, dark-twin
to mine.

7
O Non-Native—ndn—injuns! Why do you exterminate
Coyote? Hang his pelt on barbed wire, string
his ears on your belts? Do you not see how Coyote
is part of this land, the dreaming and the scheming
of Thought into Existence? Without Coyote
America would be a reservation of flat jokes
and fizzled life.

8
I grew up in Southern California where rivers
are cement troughs and Coyote sang from Hollywood Hills.
My aunts wouldn't say they were Yaqui
because that meant death or slavery in Sonora.
So they were Mexican with an indigenous rhythm.

9
When the Conquistadors came
or the priests or the Pilgrims
or Walmart, we ran away. We ran in circles
from death in one land to death in another,
and Coyote was always there, holding our souls
in the depths of his howl.

10
At the smell of smudged sage at the powwow,
the white cop sniffed sharply, looking for some Indian
smoking weed.

11
I tried riding in a canoe and almost tipped over.
Horses scare me. My car has scars along its flanks
from spatial misjudgments as I backed out of the garage.
My kind of Indian is self-defined. It's whatever I do,
however I do it. I'm not scared of who I am.

12
Fry bread is a recent tradition. Corn is older
and part of my DNA. Corn is sacred, pollen flying
into a world turned golden. Like Coyote's fur.

13
Today lasted centuries. Coyote sits next to me,
whispering promises of survival: *mañana*. It is tomorrow
and will always be tomorrow.
Stars shine all day, forever, and we don't see them.
Our souls, whether white or ndn or Other, shine even longer.
There are more than thirteen ways of seeing anyone.

Witchery

I don't mind being a lost girl
among the hedges and vines.
Something hidden watches me,
dark eye unblinking.
There in the worming woods,
amidst leaf mold and fly amanita,
I grin and twirl, wearing a crown of dead flies,
twilight seeping from my lips.
I say your name like a curse.

Earth Day

In a pinch of soil
there are millions of bacteria.
Temperate rain forests
are only 0.3 percent of the earth.
Native earthworms died
under the weight of glaciers
in the last Ice Age.

Facts. Science. Knowledge.

Hiding in the dim forest undergrowth,
the three-petaled oxblood red
wild ginger blooms,
it's heart-shaped leaves
fragrant and shy.
But do not eat.
It has carcinogenic properties.

Knowledge. Poetry. Beauty.

Plastic bags float like jellyfish
in a humpback whale's stomach.

Reality. Knowledge. Death.

Six percent of the Earth is covered by lichens,
growing inside stone, on tree bark,
on walls. They're some of the oldest
living beings, have micro worlds
existing inside and can survive in space.
They're also bio markers of environmental distress.
Some live drifting in the wind.

Knowledge. Survival. Ancient.

The Kadupul flowers once a year
moon- white in the darkest hour
and withers before dawn.
In the Blue Mountains of Oregon,
the largest organism in the world
sprawls over four square miles.
The *Armillaria ostoyae* fungus
is almost 9,000 years old.

We know so little of our world.
Ignorance. Change. Extinction.

Twenty and One

Who gathers seaweed on the fog-pebbled shores?
Who walks the autumn fields into the twilight shroud?
Who is silent when the poppy bursts its orange into the sun?
Who dwells in the painted rocks?
Who laughs when the dragonfly dances?

Where does the white go after the apple blossoms fall to the grass?
Where does the deer stand in its dappled shadow?
Where does the water dream itself into rain?
Where does the moon cry when the lemon trees outshine it?
Where do the stars sleep when you sweep your porch?

Why does the light call itself amber and not sky stalactite?
Why does Hope swing on a pendulum?
Why does the drunk driver survive the crash unharmed?
Why does your absence feel like a wound without a scar?
Why is the last door the one you're afraid to open?

What is that word in your mouth, unspoken and bitter as rind?
What is the passion you never had, the one which makes your fingertips shiver?
What is the name of the bird hidden in your shadow?
What is the sadness in purple-blue feathers?

What sonata is the fountain playing?

In the photo of our last life together, our souls share the same smile.

From *Seattle Zine*

Yesterday it didn't rain. Children were frightened. We found Aunt Martha curled on the sidewalk, desiccated. People tried to self medicate with bottles of water and wandered aimlessly, scrapping moss off their skin, muttering about The End Days.

Today it's raining again. Our gills are fully functioning. Aunt Martha is stretched out on top of the lawn like a fat sausage, singing, her voice gurgling like water down the drain pipe. She might be drowning and calling for help. It's hard to tell.

Most of us feel relief in the familiar. Rain is a lover's caress which sometimes feels like a slap on the cheek. We know the Universe loves us. But sometimes it just seems to piss on us instead. Rain is a tarot card featuring a woman with webbed hands swimming as she walks to her car.

Rain is the wet dreams of clouds.

Tomorrow, sun is forecast. There might be revolutions as the earth steams. When the sky is endless, people feel emboldened to become greater than themselves.

We shall see. Literally. With sunglasses.

A Poem Not about the Bear

Behind me I heard his teeth clacking
gnashing and smelled his meaty oily stink.
I'd seen him before, cinnamon colored
erect on two feet, front claws raking the sky.
He'd shattered my beehives, trampled
frames and scattered combs.
But that day, I didn't face him.
I walked on, skin tight, waiting
for the heavy weight of death
yet calm, knowing it wasn't him.
I walked on, past a divorce,
and close calls on a motorcycle.

But this poem is about a queen's slipper,
Cypripedium reginae.
It grows from rhizomes
spreading their fat toes underground.
The sepals are moon white,
the voluptuous lower pink lip
like Scarlett Johansson's.
I found one plant, just one,
on thirteen forested acres.
It wasn't supposed to be there
or anywhere in the western USA.
Rare as a single star in the night sky
its pale halo glowed singularly
below cedars and Douglas firs.
I walked by it daily, squatting to see
the immigrant, the impossible flowering.

The day after the bear,
I went to see the orchid.
It was smashed, the deep pink cup
smeared under the bear's paw print.
But this poem isn't about the bear.
A week later a truck backed over the track
churning its wheels in mud.
This isn't about the truck, either.
They were passing shadows.
The orchid roots felt the weight of bear and truck
and later rose against the muck,
rebounding, sending hair-like roots
from nodes, stretching laterally
into the loam. A pale bud
trembled into
the cedar-red bark
and burst translucent
in the summer rain.

Black Crows on Green Cedar

> after "Black Stone Lying on a White Stone," by Cesar Vallejo

I will die in Seattle on a rainy day
which could be any day but it's Monday
and it's raining. I'm supposed to remember dying on a day
with dreams of amber necklaces and old yellow dice
in my hands. Don't step away—my breath still fogs
the mirror. I'm so angry the doctor didn't set my arm
and there's a hill in it. My fingers walk up the hill, so tired,
and the day hasn't even begun to release its birds.
The horizon is rain.
All the yesterdays were offerings of rain.
Black crows huddle on green cedar.
Anita Endrezze is dead and in the garden
glistening stones are piled like hearts.
Her name is the gloaming. Her name is the last rose.
She left on the main road, the one with rain in its name.

Heron, Flying

It shoves off the pine branch,
legs dangling like kite strings.
Unfolding its origami wings,
it stretches a prehistoric neck,
a pterodactyl of awkward grace,
squawking
eyeing the dappled sea,
the cobbled shallows.

Crows in Color

Black crow
swaying
on a red branch.

A calligraphy of crows
on a wet ink sky.

Black crows
nesting
in green clouds.

Crow plucking
magenta magnolias.

A cauldron of crows
boiling in the blue wind.

Their dark eyes
look deep
into my brightness.

Iridescent crows, you are The Bird
as we are The Rainbow People.

Twilight of the Dreams

in which I transpose "cockroach" with "dreams"

Dreams live in a wide range of environments around the world
They prefer warm conditions found in buildings
of the human skull.
Dreams are mainly nocturnal; a peculiar exception is the Asian Dream
which is attracted to light.

The True Death's Head Dream (found in Germany during WW2)
The Smoky-brown Lucid Dream (occurs during mental fugue)
The Leapdream (which jumps from dreamer to dreamer)

Most dreams are about the size of a thumbnail
but some can be larger than the space they occupy.
One way to avoid them is to place an inch of water
in stale beer. The dreams will drown
but this method only works for American dreams,
not for German ones which are, presumably,
accustomed to dregs of leftover lager.

The Peruvian Dubia Daydream (attracted to Inca flute music)
The Brown-banded Brown Study (common in Philosophy majors)
The False Death Head's Nightmare (often found in Neo-Nazis)

Some of the earliest writings about dreams
encouraged using them as medicine.
Dreams were ground with oil
and ingested for those with insomnia.
In the 1870s, New Orleans residents
sipped boiled dream tea
to incite their urge to wander.

The Madagascar Courting Hissing Dream (often found in wet dreams)
The Bark (Canine specific)
The Flying Asian Dream (related to Kung Fu Visual Effects DreamWorks)

Because dreams are so resilient,
Russian scientists sent one into space

where it gave birth to the first non-terrestrial nightmare.
In Kafka's *The Metamorphosis,* a man is transformed overnight
into a monstrous creature with dream-like features,
including tough protective wings and leg spines.
In the music video for "Between Angels and Insects,"
dreams make numerous appearances,
most notably on a bridge
where nightmares come out
of Jacoby Shaddix's mouth when he screams.

April

Before dawn, song releases
the birds into the light,
and spring unfolds
blade and leaf unfurled
moss greening.
The world doesn't care about violins
or canvas. We can dance the rites of spring,
weaving ribbons around a phallic pole
and hide patterned eggs,
but it would go on without us.
Bright streams of birds flying north
and the sun warming roots,
the sky a violet crack amidst fading stars.

rain the rain

rain the flowering wind
the blanching moon
the cedars kneeling
in greening pools

rain the shadows
rocks steaming
the speckled sea
cloud dreaming

rain the blue
the freckled fields
the upturned face
of orca leaping

rain the ferns
the river's gulping
engulfing spitting
the trout foam spinning

rain the umbrellas
flooding streets
tendrils of hair streaming
the child's boots lemon yellow

rain the fanning clouds
the dark bruised sky
the squall water-knifing
gulls screaming

rain the puddles
the downpour filling
tree bark mossy slick
snail shell wetly shellacked

rain the incessant drumming
morning singing
the rain the rain the rain
fulcrum of fog

rain the soggy socks
the muddy floors
the spongy mop
and stinking dog

rain the buttercup
the strangling vines
the salal and wild berry
the thumb-sized frog

rain the rain
the rain the rain
rain raining
rain the rain

13 Ways to Not Write a Poem

1
Stare out the window.
The sky riding a crow's wings.

2
Stare out the other window.
Red camellias burning.

3
Tap my finger on my chin.
I used to be skinnier.

4
Play Scrabble on my iPad.
Maybe the words will stimulate my writing.

5
Play Words With Friends on my iPad.
I lose.

6
Yell at my daughter to make tea.

7
Write nothing:
a minimalist poem.
She forgets the tea.

8
Watch TV. Crime show.
Not inspiring but an hour goes by.

9
I murder a poem.
Delete.

10
Wonder if it's lunch yet.

11
I read Li Po. A gate covered with moss.
I can relate.
In Seattle, even the moon is mossy.

12
But a poem is as scarce as a Chinese monk,
his yard empty except for bird tracks.

13
An eagle flies by, squirming poem
in its talons.
Not all poems are meant to live.

Dear poem,

I've known you for a long time.
I didn't like you at first; fiction was my love
and you liked drag racing across the sheet,
and dancing iambic to Cher.

Still, there was something about you.
But I didn't want to make a commitment.

I started hanging out with other poems.
Some were pretentious, ego-written.
Others had defiant inky black tears.
I know you got jealous.

So did fiction, who waited up all night
for me to come back. I packed and left.

When we finally got together, poem,
I discovered I had to do all the work.
You just laid there, complaining
about enjambment. I didn't want sonnets.

I was all for free verse. It was the '60s, baby.
We were a couplet, trying to have the same end rhyme.

We went to college and I cheated on you
with an older cinquain. You decided to dally
with a girl named Sally at the back of an alley.
After much soul searching, we changed our POV.

We got back together. Again and again,
you ever the metaphor, me the simile.

We argued and I threw pens at you. You ignored me,
then we made up and we became a tercet.
We married, never blissfully
but our little one liners kept us together.

One grew up to be a flash fiction.
The other is a lyricist.

Now we're celebrating our 50th,
and although there were years we felt alone
and abandoned, we always believed
in the vows we exchanged, the power of words

to transform reality and unite imagination
with image and thought. Forever yours,

Anita

Poem in a Pocket

At night
with tepid stars
eyeing me
I call myself Elena
which surprises the moon.
The stars
are used to one identity
as they travel
the galaxy.

Pockets always have a menu.
They see me
inside me. They see
the wreck that I am.

Grief.
We see in each star
a molten crematoria,
orbiting souls home
to the sun's pocket.

Pretty, in two tongues
is my new name: Elena
the Electric.
I am a rosy ouzel
milky way dipper,
the pocket-less Eye.

Sometimes I sway drunken
and naked, skin hot
with volcanic dreams,
portable galaxies
ravishing my pores.

We see we are chosen vessels.
The magnetic raga
ignites a beautiful spell
over all
night's tarnished tin
stars.

My Own Oneness

>after "Paris, October 1936" by Cesar Vallejo
>Everett, April 2014

I plan on leaving
this chair, this pebbled sky. I go away
from my legs, their watery weakness.
Husband, you washed my skin
not knowing it wasn't me. I return
this flesh to the Great Obscurity.
I'll be singular, the one who leaves
 sickness on her own terms.
Counting the white pills, I will hold my hand out
for the last time, opening my mouth to the light
and swallow thirty moons.
From the streams I walk away,
and from the cedars, ferns and shells.
I resemble the rain in my death
which gives me many names
and you, my love, know them all.

Why I Don't Have Tattoos

There is no expanse of skin
as endless as your lover's. The wide plains
where fingers gallop from dark freckle to ravines
with secret dens that soft snouts burrow into.
If there were inked hills, he'd be lost
in terrain named. I want my lover to plant his flag
in lands he explores without hint of previous expeditions.
I want skin he can write his name on with his tongue.
There is a space on my right shoulder than needs wings—
 not ink, only feathering breath. And on my left buttock,
no girly butterfly. Just skin, lumpy and plump, ready for hands
to knead and squeeze. No bar codes, unicorns, or roses.
Let my skin be a book without words, a kite made of sky,
water with no shores, just oceans of pleated moist skin,
unfolding fans of female desire.

A Teaspoon of Life

I was never a recipe for disaster.
I didn't drink or cuss.
I read books
about drunk
wall-eyed women
and admired their wild hair
and lip stick smeared mouths
that seemed to swallow life whole.
I didn't stir
the air, arms akimbo, bare legs
like eggbeaters.
I didn't taste the sweet
or the bitter.
I observed, ever the writer.
Yes,
I sampled that green- eyed man,
the other with an al dente accent,
and the one who inventoried
my body parts
like an accountant.
But never the chef,
who could've cupped,
enfolded
skin to tongue
adding fluids
to steamy hot flesh.
I needed a gourmand
to teach me how
to let go and gorge myself
in lusty life.
I was never a decadent
chocolate mouthful.
I was oatmeal.
Chaste toast.
Lime without the tequila.
A page with measured words.

Relativity

Near me, a dog barks, muffled by the dark.
Somewhere you sit, book on your lap,
a robe of yellow light gracing your shoulders
and you pause
mid-sentence
thinking you heard a dog scratching at your door.
Steam rises from your cup.
I hear an owl. You hear an owl.
We are mountains
and rivers away
but reading
the same sentence.

No One Wants to Talk about This

First I threw away the pills.
Considered ties, shoelaces, bed sheets, knives.
But one has to draw the line somewhere.
Everything is a possible ending.
Step off the cliff
of a curb and a bus takes you
to the route's end.
Swallow my health supplements
and choke to death on fish oil.
I dream of walking again without falling.
I'm no star with glowing path.
I bruise and break my way in this air.
Life is the nightmare
I never wake from.
But there's always hope of a cure,
a small toad-like hope.
So I live in the fear,
the coward's fear,
of living.

Short of Life

Wheelchair-bound
I sit
every day
the African violet blooms
on a shelf
reminding me
that beauty is not a verb.

Lessons My Mom Taught Me

1: The rules
When you're in a fight, knuckle up
but keep your thumb untucked.
Back to the wall. Hit first.

Don't let a boy touch you.
Be armored. Wear bra, slip, garter belt.
Don't get pregnant.

2: from which they came
She grew up in Butte, an Italian
in WWII, near the red light district.
Her mother was absent, nursing others.
Her dad was working in Alaska, Hawaii.

She was lonely. So when the sailor danced,
holding her close, whispering I love you,
she let down her guard and unfastened
the hooks and eyes and didn't see.

3: and the consequences
She never told us about the baby
but my nana told me before she died.

His name was John. Because of him
mom was scorned by her parents

and she coldly told us girls
to keep our legs together.

We thought she was a prude.
We were teens in the free love 60s.

We didn't know the pain
of giving up a son, her life long

secret that kept her heart fisted
against the world that didn't have her back.

The Train Wreck of Love

My heart is burning alive
for you.
The Van Gogh stars are spinning for you.
The trees are greening the sky
for you, moths circling the flame for you.
The moon howls your name,
crickets are silent for you.
I hold a tin can to my ear
and hear the deep male thunder dancing for you.
In the river, tiny hearts battle upstream
for you. Clouds become deltas
for you. Trains divide the air into whistle and poem
for you, hurdling across the yellow wheat plains,
lost in tunnels that praise the darkness of you.

Birds and storming violins find their songs for you.
Oceans flood the red hills for you,
longing to touch that which is opposite.
Passion and ice. My heart burns,
my heart burns. I offer you the terrible gift of love
the fractional annihilation of self.
I offer my torn and bleeding heart
on love's altar. I offer the atlas of my body.
For you, I offer the name of my lost angel.

November

Sun on red leaves
My wheelchair lurching over
cracked pavement.
I wear pale grey and white stripped gloves.
Hedges taller than the sky
remind me that I'm only here
for a brief time. Geese fly,
old friends write,
the sky is full
of devotion.

Somewhere It's Night

The train wails a longing
for arriving.
Snow geese fly with stars
on their wings.
I'm awake at three a.m.
My life is a long night,
and I've loved a thousand moons
and some were dark.
And others lit my way
when I was lost.
Somewhere night winds
tear cherry blossoms
and they fall to holy earth.
Somewhere it's night,
and the piano is playing
a passage to dawn.

Small Space

I'm my own small space
and there's meaning
in that   Yet
what's inside of me is oceanic
forty teaspoons of salt
sweating love
(tiny fish-shaped tears)

Twenty-three feet of convoluted coils
digesting (oatmeal and pizza)

Ninety-nine percent carbon (diamond eyes)
oxygen and hydrogen
(O the weight of an earthbound soul
who longs to breathe clouds)
nitrogen and calcium
phosphorus
My bones weigh four lbs.
broken and age-porous
(sister to the dying coral)

It's crowded in here, a jelly bean jar
full of 37.4 trillion cells,
and universes of microbes surfing those cells.
(I am a cosmos of infinite beings)

My rib cage is an altar to my heart
(light the candles of love)
My pelvic bones an earthy cradle
(children slept there)

Each of my eyes has a blind spot
where the retina attaches
but my eyes see past the hole
(the way we see tree branches
and not the sky between)

I can see ten million colors
the crow's iridescent wing
turquoise veins in a rock I hold
(red willow twigs in blue rain)
the pink flush of a lover's skin

Albert Einstein's eyes are in NYC
in a safety deposit box
(mine are in a medicine woman's dream)

My hair is strong enough to support two elephants
(if ever I needed to twist a rope
and ask them to stand on it like acrobats)

Some knew my secret roses
when I was worshiped (a brown goddess)
I was young, my body a river of desire
Now, I'm a clay vessel and earth
calls to sovereign earth
This small body will mother
the dawn songs of a forest of birds

I'm everywhere
Fifty percent of the dust in my home
is yesterday's me

(the way a light bulb
doesn't confine light)
the space of me
is beyond me

I'm the space between the muscle
and the synapse, the word
that is a poem

A Symmetry of Eyebrows

Toshie Kawakami
had one hair
that was six-inches long
and two brows
shaped like
ceremonial Odachi swords
honoring the nose

avenues of skin mites
the quizzical query
runic envoys

plucked one by one
anorexic worms

or redrawn
like the mustaches
of mariachi singers

the topography of
an arched eyebrow
maps the contours
of wonder

pierced and defaced
with silver warts
or maybe pill bugs

Frida's unibrow
Mona Lisa's no brow

in the 1700s, mouse skin
was used to fill brows

two anvils
where ideas are forged
archives of aha!

waxed, tattooed
cowlicks or thick curls
where hedgehogs hide

brows: eels oscillating
to the safety of nostrils

my own are twin tables
where worries
sit and fret.

How to Taste Chocolate

1
I prefer dark chocolate
for its slightly bitter taste.
My edible life.

2
I am Ixcacoa, Little Chocolate Woman,
your sister-goddess. With such tenderness
I offer my body, the spicy brown elbows
and caramel thighs, the red wrapped heart.
The wanton self-sacrifice of love.

3
Touch your tongue
to the night, the velvety sweetness
the tiny star brickles
and white chocolate moon.

4
Chili flavored, mint, sea salt.
Lavender, cherry, orange.
Pick one and go sit on a hill.
There are the windy birds swirling
across the broken sky.
And you're sipping tea
from a thermos cup,
dissolving
lavender fields.

The Lost Umbrellas

    for Al Young and his lost umbrellas

On the horizon storm horses
stampede, cloudy manes amass
and hooves thunder. You pick up
blue umbrella, tuck paperback
into pocket, and dash to the bus,
then lightning flashes, but you're safe
inside although your skin is spurred
and you feel like you've ridden
a bucking mustang out the gate.
Thumbing pages of that western,
you fall enthralled, into panoramas
of sage and covered wagons,
shoot outs. So when your stop arrives
you fumble into reality, umbrella forgotten
as you stumble out where taxis vamoose,
glass towers are higher than saguaros
and your boss awaits with daily noose,
the hangman's grimace on his face.

Somewhere you lost that red umbrella,
the one reason you fell in love with her.
She rode a dark horse bareback
astraddle, her long hair streaming
like rain   an infinite horizon
and your heart thundered.
When you walked to the river later,
the red umbrella bobbed above,
her head leaning on your shoulder.

We have many horizons.
The day you lost the black umbrella
was when that fella backed into your auto
and you jumped out, angered, door slammed,
ham-fisted, ready to tear his head off.
It was raining. The roads slick.
And you fell, heels up. He knelt,
felt the blood pool, sticky red

from the gash on your head.
Until the ambulance came
he sheltered you with that umbrella
rummaged
from the backseat of your damaged car
and he was the calm horizon,
the edge of the known world.
When you were loaded into the van,
he sadly held the forgotten umbrella.
On his hand he'd jotted your number
but the ink wept in the rain,
dissolving in a black puddle.

Under the green umbrella, all horizons
are lost, the fabric sky-broad.
It's ridiculous, really. Why buy
such a jumbo umbrella? I thought, if ever
there was a sonnet loving
lover, we'd encompass an ever-fixed mark,
under its marriage of true minds.
We'd wander down misty paths,
breathing the same air, quoting poems
written by candlelight.
Romantic shit.
Instead, some dude groped me and I hit
him in the balls with furled umbrella
poked him in his rabbit face, spokes jabbed,
until he babbled, bent over,
and crab-walked away,
and I stood, panting, torn umbrella
bent and tattered as my dreams.

The Sacred Dissolving

    after "Deshojacion Sagrada" by Cesar Vallejo

The moon goddess is immensely forgotten
by men digging oily pits they call
by company name.
The red crown of Jesus is elevated to stone
while her sacred emeralds are ground into dust.
Above the blue heavens there is more blue,
blue like wine poured into the sea, like the veins
of a blue-skinned goddess, like the lips of
the strangled feminine. Mother Earth,
Mother Moon!
Into the holocaust you have been thrown,
your opal gypsy heart burned to ashes
by vagrant, desperate men who cry sad songs
and don't know why.

The Secret of Black

There's the kettle, its anger against the pot
sputtering with sizzling spit upon the rim.
And the pot which calls itself
dainty, filling itself with lies of honey
or tea, damp leaves that tell the future
of bitter secret quarrels.

There's the cat, with its twitching tail,
defining darkness with her whiskers. She arches
her back, sleek fur shining
like rippling night. Black
is every paw fall, each step quick on the curious
earth. And in her dreams, black curves
its wicked claws over the humped-back rat,
the dark bird that quivers weakly.

Black is all colors combined. The words on this page
disappear into night when you close the book.
Black comes from *scorched*, *burn*, a *flash* of light before
the darkness takes your hand and strips it to the bone.
If Black had a secret, it would be unknown. A mouth
without a tongue. Your name with no body.

The Secret of Balloons

Hydrogen was our father.
Ballet was our mother.
We dance out of reach
or hang on trees like hollow fruit.
Our secrets go with us,
all that emptiness
inside. Like you.
Is your secret contained in a small balloon
of silence, ready to be popped with the prick
of your tongue?
You are oxygen and hydrogen, carbon, and salts.
You float through your lives, encased in colorful skins.
You make secrets and keep them. You let them go
with strings attached. Your hearts are no ballasts;
only dark secrets, those dirty fists of lies,
tether you to this earth.
If you were to release all your secrets,
all those heavy words,
you would rise, rise, rise
into the horizon, free. Bewildered.

Collections

A *fetish* of shoes: pumps and stilettos,
soft matte leather flats, plastic jellies, rubbers and sling backs.
Wedgies and mules, sandals and slippers.
Shoes hate a jumbled closet floor. They need to stomp, click,
pound and roam. They need each other and the foot within
they call Wanderlust. Bejeweled, strapped, buckled, and shiny—
shoes march, parading their owner's *want   want   want* .

A *wake* of buzzards.
A *shuffle* of bureaucrats.
A *sneer* of butlers.
A *prolix* of poets.

A *bebe* of dolls: bisque, ball-jointed.
Paper dolls with tender necks. Wood faces
with painted mouths, rosy cheeks.
Reborn baby dolls with skin softly human,
lips pursed to cry *Mama!*   Who collects dolls?
The lonely woman. The girl who mothers
herself. The couple who desperately
search for a porcelain child
to buy on eBay.

A *hootchie-kootchie* of harlots.
A *glaze* of windows.
A *body* of morticians.
A *hustle* of beggars.

Collections of stamps, coins, Beanie Babies,
vintage gloves, hats, first editions, signed volumes,
vinyl records, tea cups, string, bottle caps,
guns, lovers, comic books, shells, buttons.
The secret of a collection
is that it collects
you.

Noon

I loved him when the sun was an immense
field of broken stems, light
flashing from the mirrors of leaves.

I loved him when the hand turned over
and the palm of midnight
caressed me with dark fingers.

If you can love a man in the glare
of day when his faults are as visible
as your own, then tomorrow will be twofold.

Now and *Forever*. Such constant longing!
Time stands still in lovers' hearts.
Their hungers crave eternity.

Noon stands on ballerina pointe,
a slim faceless girl with no shadow.
Noon is mute,

all secrets enfolded, waiting for day
to open like a fan, or a switchblade.
Then the spell is broken, the air hisses

and the birds rustle. The man discovers
that love is both sun and shadow.
O, I loved him once. When I was young

and true promises seemed possible.
My lips bruised easily, swollen
from kissing. I beguiled him,

with my slender arms and flashing eyes.
When noon arced and passed, my passion cooled.
I left him. I took my secret

places with me, that intimate dusky flesh
and shameless tongue,
this restless heart.

Cup

Its empty or it is not.
When its full, it understands
its purpose. It knows it has a soul
and that God has a plan for it.
When it's empty, it understands
that nothing is still something.
A soulful cup can be full of sustenance,
giving of itself to others.
The cup can reflect on its shape,
the hollowness that allows
itself to be filled. That's its secret;
void or replete—its duality
is the same.

Roof

Here, the stars find pasture.
The Moon taps on the tiles
with its bright hammer.
Birds sleep like stones,
heads curled under wings
so motionless—
tiny bones weigh down
the roof's longing to fly.

Day and the birds
glow like topaz and brush stardust

from roofs. The sky embraces
its own language of the tops of things:
the white sky of snow, the child's head,
the mountainous roofs of the world.
Here, is the roof's secret: that all is
under its humble protection.
And so we sleep and pray and die
under roofs of tile or stars or rain.

Passing

For Terry Farrell

On the other side of the sky,
the moon burns.
Ashen moonlight dusts
my eyes. At dawn
I hold the sea
shell in my hand.
The tide pulls
my soul away from shore.
Birds the secret colors of roses
follow me as I drift,
calling me back to the roots,
those immense doors,
opening, opening.

Circle

With my lips I seek the circle's secret,
the shape of tongue grooved against teeth,
words caught in the cage of my mouth.
I'm silent. The circle is whole. It does not need me
to complete itself.
The circle keeps its secret
unbroken.

The Tunnel's Secret

There is a sky at the end of its neck.
And dark heat above it or oceans over it.
There are minerals and gems embedded in it,
green salamanders and red snakes.
Concrete or tiled or bricked
the tunnel, buttressed with tree muscles,
is a sleeve of darkness.
It has one eye like a glass jewel, glowing
or jet black. It has one direction,
whether coming or going.
It has two secrets, the ins and outs
of whys and hows.
It's a tube, a wormhole, the distance between
life and death. Ancestors gather there
to welcome us, roads take us
farther away from loved ones.
Fog floods in and moonlight
laces the mouth.
Tunnels pull in the wind, whistling
the long lonely destinies of trains.
There are empty cores in all our lives,
tunnels to be filled in and followed,
passages to intimate secrets and shame
channels riddled with mysteries.

A Circle Can't Have Corners

1
The nose is a corner,
right angle to the eyes
that can't see it.
Yet the nose exists.

The red rose is an endless circle
of petals, blooming on the horizon,
like a perfumed sun.

We stumble against Life's dark edges,
but believe there is something
beautiful as a crimson petal,
beyond our vision.

2
On the anniversary
of our deaths, we turn the corner,
come full circle.

We see what was there all along.

The moon drops its waxen petals
on the last cornerless path
and our eyes blink in wonder
at the broad holy way,
the red road,
before us.

A Poem Found in a Dream

God: I have come from my galaxy
into your world:
an ocean into a thimble.

Night Psalm

The world around sends up its holy chant
    from "A Night Psalm," by Slovenian National Poet Oton
    Zupancic (1878-1949)

In the soft summer twilight, pale blue
horses float through moonlight.
This far north, night falls late
and incomplete.
Robins sing slower at midnight
while ivy grows an inch,
tendrils tangling stars.

If you're far from home, lost,
and the tide of war is rising,
and your dreams
have stuttered slow,
and the world's fist
is a body blow
against your tenderness,
be the resolute ivy.

Be the light that lingers
in the darkness.
Be that holy chant
in the robin's song,
the waves rippling,
in the fragrant dawn.

The Secrets of Time

Time: the invisible trespasser of our lives.
Time has no ending. Is Time a pillar of years?
How many hearts does Time have?
Time is God's last creation.
Does Time peel like an onion?
Time is the salt on the meat of existence.
What is Time's past life?
Is Time a world of itself?
Time never sleeps, yet it dreams.
Is Time destiny?
Is Time a river or a pomegranate?
Time looks like a whirlwind. Or an egg.
Does Time remember you?
Is Time the universal language of our planet?
Time is gravity; it weighs on your hands.
Time is a mad dog.
Does Time have a shadow?
Do the wild geese time their migration to when the sky is the color of tears?
Is Time human?
Time is the bone of eternity.
Is Time a melody or a drum beat?
Does Time rise like yeast?
Einstein is a descendant of Time.
At birth you were sentenced to life without parole.
Time takes too long.
Is Time more like an onion or perfume?
Time is revenge.
Is your life a Time capsule?
Are you Time-worn?
Is Time the first red leaf of autumn?
Time is like a sad elephant without memory of its present existence.
Is Time a relative of yours?
Is your life a Time bomb?
Time is a shell game. And it is watching you.
Does Time have the last word?

Anita Endrezze is a writer, poet, teacher, and artist. Her writing has appeared in many literary magazines and in dozens of anthologies, such as *Carriers of the Dream Wheel, Harper's Anthology of Twentieth Century Native American Poetry, Reinventing the Enemy's Language, Talking Leaves, Blue Dawn, Red Earth, Earth Song, Sky Spirit,* and a book of autobiographical essays, *Here First.* She is the author of eight books including the short story collection, *Butterfly Moon; Throwing Fire at the Sun, Water at the Moon; at the helm of twilight; Bjerget og Skystaanden;* and *Lune d'Ambre.* She also has two chapbooks of poems, *Breaking Edges* and *A Thousand Branches.* Her work has been translated into ten languages (Farsi, Danish, French, German, Macedonian, Italian, Portuguese, Chinese, Catalonian, and Spanish). A recent broadside from Red Bird Press features her poem "K.I.A.," along with artist James Autio. Her collaborative altered-book projects have toured the world, with one archived in the Smithsonian Institute. Some of Anita's paintings can be found on book covers, such as *Harper's Anthology of Twentieth Century Native American Poetry.* She's had exhibitions in England, Wales, and the U.S.A.

Endrezze has a Master of Arts Degree in Creative Writing from Eastern Washington University, and a B.A. in English with an emphasis on Secondary Education. She's taught high school, college, university, and in the Poets in the Schools program. She's won the Washington State Writers Award, the Bumbershoot/Weyerhaeuser Award, an Artist Trust Gap Award, and First Place in the Washington Poetry Society Contest. She was a two-year appointee for the Washington State Humanities Commission in their Inquiring Mind Speaker series. Anita speaks Danish and some Spanish. Anita is half-Native American (Yaqui, Pima, Maya), Slovenian, north Italian, German-Swiss.

www.ingramcontent.com/pod-product-compliance
Lightning Source LLC
LaVergne TN
LVHW041345080426
835512LV00006B/615